Some things I still can't tell you

Some things I still can't tell you

Poems

Misha Collins

Andrews McMeel
PUBLISHING®

For West and Maison,

May you grow happy and strong. You are loved more
than any silly book could ever explain.

Contents

Love poems

THE KISS

The longest kisses
Were some of the first.
In high school, we sat on the east lawn hill
By the student center.
There's a picture, me lying on my back,
You straddling me, marking property
On that lawn, in your blazer,
With our friends sunning nearby.

I remember lying face-to-face
Breathing your breaths,
Mouths open, lips joined,
Breathing out as you breathed in.
Our stomachs pressed,
Mine rising as yours receded,
Inhaling to exhaling
Used air.

Did we deprive ourselves of oxygen?
Did we kill brain cells?
Would we have scored higher on the SATs
If we hadn't been so in love?

This morning, decades later, in our ultra-chic kitchen
You disappeared into the living room, saying:
"I'm going to leave you to work out your own bad mood.
I'm not going to wait around for you to take it out on me."
When I couldn't see you anymore,
I called out,

"Don't leave me like that. Be nice before you go."
And you came straight back and leaned down
And kissed me with still, pursed lips,
And we held our mouths together for the longest time
Before peeling back to start our days.

LEG WRESTLERS

I remember getting to know you
As a body in my bed.
I don't mean that way,
Or at least not just that way;
I mean learning to sleep
Next to someone else.
We used to spool the duvet
Around ourselves,
Leaving the other uncovered,
And you'd drool
On my shoulder,
On the pillows,
On anything you could
Get your sleeping lips on.
But the main thing I remember
From sleeping in the
Getting-to-know-you years
Was our war for
Vertical dominance,
Who'd flop their leg on top
And who'd be the
Pinned-down underdog.
In later years, we'd be content
Under or over,
As long as some
Leg-flopping was going on.
I remembered this last night in bed
When my knee crept up the hotel wall,
Looking for you as I tried to sleep.

A MEAL OF BEETS

Last night, we ate beets
Raw and warm, with rice and greens,
An avocado, and a broken head of garlic
In a wooden bowl between us,
Our faces lit by a drooping, half-melted candle.

You said eating like this reminded you of
Our summer in Washington:
All the vegetables, slow and nowhere to go.

Then from your office you brought a note
On one of those torn half-sheets
That you write to me on planes from time to time.
You dropped the folded page beside my plate,
Pinked with beet and a few grains of scattered rice.

I leaned in toward the candle across our table,
To your adoring eyes, and read these words,
Written while you were crying at a window seat.

Now—after seventeen years,
Four cities, shared partners, pregnancy scares,
And so many things that add up to two lives already lived,

Reading your note, at our table, in my voice,
I heard you were ready to accept my love,
Which, of course, changes everything.

THE MOTHER OF LEARNING

"Paftarenya mat oocheniya"
 Is Russian for:
"Repetition is the mother of learning."
 There are parts of your body
 That I replay in my mind
 Like a scratch on a vinyl record,
 The needle of my memory
 Returning again and again
 To the same part of you,
 Repeating and repeating
 Until your contours are
 What I know best,
 What I love most.

SUN AND SHADOW

Last night, Saint Patrick's Day out on a rainy street,
I got a call from you.
We complimented each other for having
Told the truth,
For having that to count on
All these years.

And then you explained how you'd discovered
That San Francisco streets always have a sunny side
And a shady side,
That back in LA the buildings were so spread
That both sides are sunny,
And in New York, the buildings are so tall
That it's shade, shade, shade, except at high noon.
You said you hoped you would get a chance
To show me the one-side-sunny-other-side-shady thing;
You hoped I would come back with you and see the light,
And I told you you melted me.

Then in front of me, a woman with a shamrock hat yelled,
"Stop, you fucker!" to a passing cab,
And I said to you, "I'm freezing," which I was,
And that I had to go inside.
"Inside where?"
"Just a café," I lied,
As I opened the door to a tanning salon.
There are some things I still can't tell you.

A FIVE POINT EIGHT

At my desk the room sways,
And this is not a boat.
The blinds shouldn't be swinging
With the windows shut.

I run reflexively out to the yard and
Looking in our shaking window
I see her in the sundress that I bought,
Standing in an inside doorway
In our first rocking California quake.

The lawn moves under me.
She's still frozen in the door;
I just have time to think,
"Please, God, let me have
Built this home strong enough."

When the ground steadies under me,
I find her barefoot in the kitchen.
She says she remembered "doorway";
I tell her that now they say
To get outside but that I'm glad
I got to see her hips and
Shapely silhouette from behind.

DEVIL IN THE DETAILS

When I'm far from you,
I imagine the
Details of your existence,
What you had for breakfast,
Who you saw for lunch,
Whether you have on
Your white sweater
Or your red one
On this East Coast winter day,
As if painting in
Your waking hours
With textures, tastes,
And geographies
Will make you
More real to me
And close the space between us.

LAKE OF LIFE

Last night, in the bed in the dark
There were spells of quiet,
Long stretches when she'd say nothing,
And I knew that she was crying.

Her father died a year and a half ago.
Waves of mourning still come,
Along with some regret.

She said, "But I feel like I know him
Better now that he's gone."

When I fell asleep,
I dreamt the following poem:

When you were swimming in the lake of life,
You thrashed and kicked up your head,
Your arms slapped the surface waves and water foam.
But there's a calm and glassy stillness
In the quiet of your death,
And I can see far down
To the depths of you
That I never knew to love.

JUNE SECOND

This morning, we walked outside
And the street was covered in freshly fallen Jacaranda petals:
A blanket of floppy purple snow.

I complained.
"We wait all year for these flowers,
And they're gone in a week."

"Hmm," she said,
Crushing wilted purple blossoms with her shoes.
"Hmm what?"
"I haven't been waiting for anything."

But she has.
I know it.

AM

Waking up,
There are always things
To be grateful for.
Obvious, easy things:

Like first sun climbing past
The petals of the bougainvillea
Through my bedroom window
And knocking
In patches
On my eyelids.

How could I not be thankful for that?

Or another thing,
Witnessing her sleeping cheeks
Stretch into her yawning,
I love you,
Good morning grin.

If you saw it, you'd know.
Anyone would feel lucky then.

Or the scratching of those little
Finch feet on the feeder.

I think when I hear that,
Thank God for that.

But this morning,
When I swung sitting sideways
On the edge of the bed
In that space before standing,
I found a big thing
I had been missing:

I have to remember to
Be grateful for me.

COUCH CAMPING

A morning exercise:
We've been
Saying, face-to-face,
What we love,
How we feel,
Appreciating
Me for her and
Her for me.

This morning, we put a
Knit blanket over our heads,
And on the couch,
In our cotton tent,
We stare eye to eye.
"I feel like we are an electromagnet."
"I don't know what that is."
"I don't either, but you make me feel like one."
"I loved when you kissed me
When I gave you pineapple."
That makes her cry.

When we lean in to nuzzle,
Blinded in collapsing cotton folds
Of blue knit tent,
We bump foreheads
Before finding lips.

CLASPED

I keep walking between two buildings at work today.
This February-dark day can't decide if it wants to rain
Or sleet or snow, so it's settled somewhere between
And a cold, steady, wet white lands as droplets on my sleeve.

I look up and the backlit flakes disappear
Against a wilderness of gray.
The sky is perfectly painted the color of cold.
Looking up, my open eyes are pelted from above,
And when I stop to blink and close my lids,
I suddenly see you.

Your cold and rosy rain-chapped cheeks
Reflected in the window of a city shop,
But your winter storm is in another place.
My left grabs my clenched right fist,
Yearning for your distant hands to be in mine.

SOME THINGS I STILL CAN'T TELL YOU

BROWN HENS

My wife reads to me from the guidebook
About the cheesemakers
On the island where you can see the cheese made.
We follow the map off the coast highway.

"There! Old Shelburne Road," she reads from a sign,
Her eager finger pointing.
On the farm's long gravel drive,
Her back floats just off the seat.

They have goats to pet
And windows to look through.
We can see women dressed as maids making cheese.

Tasting every sample twice,
She reads how many eggs per chicken per year.
She asks if brown hens lay brown ones.
"I don't think so," I offer.

Winding back to the coast, belly full,
She confesses:
"The book said it was for children."

27

TUG OF WOMAN

Last night, I shared a woman with a bed.
We wrestled her back and forth for hours,
The bed and I.
I started with the upper hand;
My calves wrapped her shins,
My nose pressed her neck
(Inhaling scents of suckling infancy).
"You smell like a baby," I said,
And she smiled with her shoulders.

Then our furnace of body heat
Bolstered the bed's advance,
And the sheets peeled her
From my sweating chest
And gripped her
In their damp half nelson.
And so went the night,
Tug of woman
Between a bed and me.

ZEN MORNING

We sat outside to meditate on our new used couch
By the turtle pond I made off our back porch.
Still in your underwear, you brought us blankets,
And we sat with the trickles of the fountain sounds,
Morning warming with the rising sun.
Bobbing between asleep and awake,
You lay your head on my lap.
Then, that screaming, clanging, weekly revving truck:
"Shit!" I said, "It's garbage day."
I ran flushed to the alley,
Furious at my forgetfulness.

FALL BACK

It's the first cold rain of late fall,
And for the first time, I turn on
My apartment's fireplace.
The smell of summer's dust is burning off.
My landlord says he can't find
A lightbulb that fits this room's lamp.

The clouds out the small window
And the sound of rain running down the glass,
Along with the fire,
Could add up to autumn coziness,
But in this nest, there is no you,
So all I see is damp and dark today.

THESE HOURS

I want more time,
More of you.
I want more youth,
More good years
With un-sore hips
And late-night lips.
I want to travel
Back to our beginning
So I can re-learn you
And re-earn you,
This time better.
This time, I'll savor and
Remember everything.
This time, time will
Slow down in
All the right places
And fly by when
You fly away.
This time, I'll make
Einstein's relativity
Bend to my will.
This time,
These hours will be
Our hours.

WAY-FINDING

When I met you, I was twenty pounds lighter,
An inch shorter,
And a child.

You were always full-grown
And perfect
In my child's mind.

And now we've lived a life together
With homes and jobs and even kids.
We loved one another,
We loved others,
We wondered who we were.

And now we're grown
(Perhaps not old)
And yet we still
Want to know
How to live and
How to love.

You said last night,
"What does it mean?
That you love me?"
And I'm not really sure.

All I know
Is that without you
I am lost.

THE CENTER

When I accidentally swipe right on my iPhone's home screen,
It takes me to the "control center," a serious name
For a useless function.
I never navigate there on purpose, but there it is,
Between texts and tweets from my clumsiness,
And it shows me a new photo from years ago
Featured at the top of the screen,
A picture iOS has picked for me,
With the words in white letters, "For you."
Most days, that photo is of you smiling.

Last night, my knuckles nudged the screen to the right,
And a picture popped up.
Us side by side in Bali with parrots on our shoulders.
I teared up and stupidly texted it to you.
I wrote, "I will always feel this way about you.
I will never not love you."
Retyping that now, tears again.

When I was learning to act
And needed to cry for a scene,
I would often imagine the unbearable emptiness
Of a life without you.

Hope, joy, running
& other good things

REREAD

Yesterday I read a used book
Whose previous readers
Had inexhaustible supplies
Of red and yellow ink.

Whole chapters highlighted.
Paragraphs double underlined in
Straight, red rows.

And I imagined my young fore-reader
Hunched late at a shared table
In the Portland State library,
Hiding a cold, surreptitious coffee
Between his legs,
Reading lines like,
"Be the running, not the runner."
And uncapping his red pen
Yet again,
Thinking:
"Yes, yes, that's it!
I AM THE RUNNING!"

IN PASSING

I'm alone in San Francisco.
And this morning, a man walked past me
On a steep hillside sidewalk.

I was on Grant Street, my knees pointing downhill;
I turned shoulder-front and sideways
To slip past the city shoppers,
And, in a white oxford,
Under the sheath of a shaved scalp,
The man climbed toward me,
And, passing, he said the words,
"Don't be lonely. Be HAPPY."

Not looking back, he just kept walking
Up and up toward a cable car.

He was speaking to me.
I'm sure of it.

SUDDENLY

A piece of grass,
Not a whole blade,
Just a severed piece,
Drying in the sidewalk's sun.

I walk down my jog
In a mowed afternoon,
And even here in a shard of green,
In a fragment of a thing
That is smaller than a leaf,
Even here,
The magic of this life.

WATERSHED

I've been wanting to explore my city,
Be a tourist at home
Because lately I've been curious about everything,
Even cracks in the sidewalk.

So today, a Saturday, I'm on a bus
Touring the LA River
With twenty-five curious others
Aiming digital cameras at this greasy stream,
This hot, algaic water in its long concrete trough.

Through chain-link holes we move
To the cement riverbank
With our tuna sandwiches
And learn that these mutant ducks
Escaped from Chinatown restaurants.

Sitting there, I get a voicemail from my old tenant
Saying, "I wish we could have tea again.
I wish we still lived upstairs.
I hope you're as happy as we are."
And I almost cry at her sweetness.

Later, under a broken bridge
On a sculptured heap of trash and sludge,
Our guide tells us,
"Only schizophrenics
See the beauty here."

5/7/5
INSTRUCTIONS
FROM A BOOK TITLED:
ZEN AND THE ART OF ACTING

An actor, I read,
Should wash the floor, hands and knees,
Before rehearsal.

This morning, I wiped
The tile, crawling with a sponge.
A spider ran off.

MORNING, WORLD

This morning, for no reason,
Or maybe for some territorial primate reason,
I felt compelled to open the front door
And survey my yard and street
And waking neighborhood.
I stepped into the porch roof shadow,
With the line of early sunlight
Cutting just across my toes,
The manzanita leaves quaking to the breeze.
Down the block, a banging, rolling
Delivery truck door.
And without thinking,
I said out loud,
"I love you, world."
My feet on the cold concrete.

NEGATIVITY BIAS

Years ago, I met a man at a dinner party,
A professor of literature
(We'll call him "Costya" to expose the guilty).
A fellow diner at the dinner asked about my idle time,
And I said I'd been writing some,
That I'd recently submitted poems
And that I hoped one may be printed for the public to review.
My new acquaintance, "Costya," asked,
"Why should anyone read what *you* write?"
The guests and I were slack-jawed at this cruelty,
And, shaken, I stammered to retort.

But, with time, I have reflected.
Perhaps he meant to wonder:
Did I really have a purpose or a point?
Was I wasting readers' time?
Was I typing words for ego, or trying to be smart?

And now, ten years deep, I *could* say,
"I write to shake you, my dear readers,
And wake you from your slumber,
And show you a new way!"

But the truth is, I write mostly
In the mornings, drinking tea,
And, when I write, I am writing
Mostly just for me.

And Costya, my dear Costya,
If you don't like it,
You may set this down at any time.

THE BELL CURVE

I invented a game in the tenth grade.
We would grade one another—
Not grades for tests or courses
Or even academic years,
But we'd assign letter values to
One another's whole person.

I gave an A- to Tassia
And then explained the reasons why:
She had a charming laugh and clever mind
But a bit too much self-doubt
To warrant her a solid A.

Leaning on the ping-pong table,
John, my oldest friend,
Rated me a crushing C.
"You're too much of a dreamer,"
Said he to me,
And the score has stuck.
I always think, *I'm drifting too much in my head.*

But here, rewriting old poems
By a window at my desk,
I have to say: that passing grade—
The dreamer's C—
It's good enough for me.

THE SOUND AND THE FERRY

On Lopez Island, we do not rise lazily in the morning.
Sunrise grabs us where we lie
(Outside on a mattress on a deck above the waves).
Daybreak is a drill sergeant daring us to defy it,
Yanking us from under our dew-damped sheets,
The fire of dawn raging in its irises,
Spitting sea breath so close we can taste mist,
Alarms of southbound geese blaring overhead,
And the foghorn *WAKE UP!* of a
Passing ferry in the sound.
The new day grabs us,
Shouting "rise" and "hear" and "see,"
And, springing up and looking out, we dare not disobey.

DOWNPOUR

"Time flies," an old friend told me today.
But maybe time slips through God's fingers,
Runs down His arms and legs,
And pools on the ground at His feet,
Each moment evaporating,
Condensing and falling back
To us as rain,
And the whole time, we think things like,
"Poor me,"
When instead
We could turn our bodies outdoors,
Feel the warm rain on our skin,
And watch the skies
Open for all of us.

FIRE AND WATER

Part One: Absolution

Many years ago, I got a phone call
With news that made me want to give up.
I sat and stared for an hour
And then took myself for a run
In Griffith Park, up through Little Armenia
Into the hills and chaparral.

When I rounded the liquor store,
Starting up Hillhurst, I saw plumes of smoke,
Heard sirens and helicopters, and felt hot wind.
I ran toward it all, thinking the destruction might purify me.

I passed the Greek theater and dozens
And dozens of fire trucks and hundreds of firemen
So consumed in suiting up,
Unfurling hoses, and saving structures
That none noticed a shirtless white boy bounding past.

I ran up onto a fire road
And toward the burning embers in the wind,
Pushing through near-tears and rounding an uphill turn.
A gust caught the fire's vanguard,
And I was suddenly running in a tunnel of fire
That swept over my head and across the path
And spread in every direction I looked.
I thought: This is how I die.

Just then, with a concussive pounding in my chest,
The thundering blade of a fire-fighting helicopter.
Cold and wet and steam overtook me as
I was baptized in a sooty rain of water from above.
I don't know if the pilot saw me or God did, but I felt
Reborn and washed in gratitude for this life.

Longing, sadness, running & foreboding

FIRE AND WATER

Part Two: Pyreless

More than a decade past,
Southern California is burning again.
I wake feeling broken and
Once again wonder if my park might fix me.
I run up in an amber haze, the fires distant,
But the smoke and heat are sweeping in on coastal winds.
From Dante's Peak, I see
Bright spots burning through the haze
And LA County Fire copters dropping to collect
Water from the lake that's dammed up in the hills.
Here in the park, though, I am far from water,
And I am damned.
Everything on this path is dry and hot and brown.
There's barely even wetness in my mouth.
At the peak, I stop and hold a fence post,
Light-headed from the smoke and sun and sadness.
Today, I am not absolved, I am not purified.
I am the only runner in these hills.

WATER BREAK

Running in Charlotte in a hot and sunny
Summer Sunday afternoon,
I saw an old man with a pit bull
Sitting on a lawn, brown and packed to dirt by dog's paws—
A veteran, I guessed—one leg missing at the knee.
In the sticky heat, a radio on an extension cord,
Resting on a rusted metal chair,
Funk music on cheap speakers.

I stopped. Shirtless and sweat-soaked on my run,
I pointed to his garden hose coiled in the weeds:
"Can I get a drink of water? I'm dying in this heat."
He flicked one hand to say, *Okay,*
With a screw-top Bud Light in the other.

I crossed his yard, turned the water on, and let it run
So I wouldn't taste the sunbaked rubber.
I drank and drank, then thanked him.

He asked, intently, "What brings you here?
Where you going?"
As if I were running *to* something,
Or had a purpose or a plan.
"I'm just running," I said.
But as I trotted off, his questions stuck to me.
An insistence in his tone of voice,
As if he *knew* me and needed me to ask myself,
Why am I here? Where am I going?

BLACK CAT

The other day, a cat passed through my hedge,
And I thought of a poem that would feature it,
But the poem took its course,
The hedge took center stage,
And the cat was written out of the script.

Last night, the cat came back.
A new cat in the neighborhood.
He brought two friends, one tailless
All mewing on my front porch.

A part of me thought
That the new cat knew
I had, in my poem,
Abandoned him for the leafy hedge,
And now he'd returned
With his henchmen.

When the screeching started, she
Lowered the *New Yorker* to her lap
And said, "What's going on with those cats?"
I peeled back the curtain
And saw a circle of fur.

Then, a spell of unease.
Not just the tingle of superstition
But a swelling, spinal fear
That these intruders
Might come for us in our sleep,
Take our souls and leave us cursed.

EUGENIA

In my yard, there's a kind of plant growing
All along the fence; it's called a Eugenia.
And I want it to be a hedge
That blocks the lights of the liquor store.

But my Eugenia has grown to be a hedge-like tree,
With thick trunks and high branches
That nod in breezes.
And I can see the bright neon all night long.

Then, this summer, the bark began to bald,
With leaves wrinkled, pocked, and reddish,
So a plant specialist, an enthusiast, came to advise.
"A mite has invaded California," she told me.

"We're seeing this on Eugenia all over.
 Don't worry, they've introduced a wasp,
 And the wasp will eat the mites.
 But if you want this to stay a hedge,
 You've got to cut the leaders off the top there.
 You see, your Eugenia
 Wants to be a tree."
I told her, "I want it to be a hedge."

I only wish I knew
What I wanted *me* to be.

SMOG CUTTERS

Her let-me-save-you words,
Her lying on the couch in jeans.
We have to talk, let's connect,
Fell like shovelfuls of damp earth
Burying me alive.

Later, much later, at the Thai bar alone,
As I peeled whole barbecued shrimp
And drank Long Island iced tea like Lipton
To the sound of broken-English karaoke,
My muscles felt loosed from the bone,
And I cried shoulder-shaking tears.

Amidst the scents of whiskey and gin,
The oily husking of shrimp,
And the Thai man's soul-saving song,
"West Virginia, take me home,"
The old woman who brought my drink
Touched my arm.

In the Christmas-lit bar,
As I was slipping beneath the waves of despair,
Her tender, mothering hand
Reached down and pulled me out,
And, somehow, I could breathe.

THESE DAYS

I've been doing this funny thing in the afternoons,
This going and lying down
In our bed thing,
Slightly curled on my side
In my jeans and shoes,
Staring at the back side of the blinds,
Crying.

My puffed cheek soaks our pillow
And I cry.
No known reason—
Just tears on my side,
Slightly fetal,
Hidden,
Sad to my bones.

THE EMPTY

Wine-tipsy, I crawl into the back porch guest bed,
The white duvet stiff with desert grit.
(In this windy, rainless LA summer,
You could shovel the deep dust
Off your windowsills.)

Face up and too hot to sleep,
My mind on day thoughts,
The night's city sky over-lit.
Above me, a bird taps
On the plastic roof,
Sound of a Harley revving at the bar.

I stretch my arms,
Spread my legs,
So the bed's empty space
Won't feel so big.

I, ASSASSIN

Now that summer reigns,
For days,
Itching, bloodsucking bites
From black fleas
Have welted my skin.

Hardware store.
Gas canisters.
Six hours.
Plumes of air-borne living room death.

The woman with the terrier said,
"They're in the grass in June.
You've got to
Kill them where they live."

So, the lawn too.
A toxic wash.
Oily spray.
Foam.

And then,
At my feet,
Shiny ladybugs
Running from their beds
Stumble, wings half-unfurled,
Horribly onto the flagstones.

What have I done?

IN MY HOTEL BED

At this fancy hotel, the maids wear
A bleak, white maid's frock.
They fold down the sheets at six o'clock
And put away my underwear.

Last night, in my turned-down bed,
China's Olympics on the plasma display,
My wife rang for the fourth time that day
To say, "I know it's dumb, I just miss you.

Will you play the appreciation game?"
(It's a thing she likes to do where I say
Something nice about her brightening my day,
And then in her sweet way she does the same.)

But I noticed a tightening in my chest,
A closing off and wanting rest,
So I said, "no," and read instead
A poem I had written lying there in bed.

THE WRONG ROAD

I had dinner yesterday with a dangerous woman
In a sushi restaurant. I am married, and
I could see sparkles in the makeup on her cheeks.
She told me secrets and left the tofu in her miso soup.

Dinner done, I wanted to pay and run, but
She asked me to walk her back to her hotel.
Her alone at night in a strange city, I couldn't say no.

In the lobby, she touched my arm
With forty years of loneliness.
I quickly said, "This was nice," and "Goodnight,"
And pushed hard on the revolving door,
Straining to be free.

Safe in the hotel driveway, I dropped my shoulders,
Opened my umbrella, and started for home.
Three teenagers passed.
"Hey buddy," one said, "it's not raining anymore."
I looked out at the night's street
And saw patches where the pavement
Had already dried.

My people
(& other people)

SOME THINGS I STILL CAN'T TELL YOU

THE FEELING OF BLUE

Eating broccoli at the table in our kitchen,
I was staring at the row of frying pans
Dangling from their handles,
And out of nowhere she said,
"Don't you love deep blue?"
Some silence set in and she said,
"Do you ever feel that way toward some people?
Like, Leigh is one of those people.
When I think of her, she seems so human
That I have the softest, softest sweetness toward her,
And sometimes I feel that way with strangers."

I just looked at her with open eyes,
And we weren't drunk,
And we weren't high.
(Unless steamed greens
Can make you high).

WILD FLOWER

Sunday, we drove up two hours
To see the poppies bloom
With a close friend
(An almost lover)
Who still left me tongue-tied,
Her pretty legs
Stretched across the back seat in the high desert.
She told us about rain
And why the blossoms are
Brighter some years.
Driving, I searched for words
To convey a feeling
(Maybe longing),
But nothing came.

At a gas station,
Asking directions,
I waited while a blushing man
Paid for condoms
And a Sunday *Times*.

In the car again,
Drowsing from a sleepless night,
I thought of all the things I didn't say,
Until we crested a sandstone ridge
And all at once, curving to the downhill side,
The blinding California poppies
Swept the desert valley

In orange and green
As far as we could see.
Finally finding my words,
I said, "Look.
Look at all those flowers."

ALESSANDRA

I saw her in the airport last year
Looking just the same.
We traded emails, and I
learned her new last name.

This weekend, dressed smartly,
I found the place early and ordered a big bottle
Of sparkling water. She came late,
Kissed both cheeks, and ordered "still."

We shared chestnut chicken and aubergine,
A linen-serviced Chinese lunch in London.
Her American dialect was clipped and neat;
She didn't glottalize her *t*'s.

She's friends, she said, with Bill and Hillary
But had a recent falling out with
The ambassador to France.

Her bangs were the same, and somehow
She got me talking about my mother
Like she used to, when we sat in the stone-walled
Bedroom of our freshman dorm.

"I just know I *need* to be successful," she declared.
As I balanced my chopsticks on a chestnut on my plate,
I thought of all the sadness in that phrase,
And how I once was tempted by this woman and her yearning
For what she couldn't have.

THE COMMUTER

I have a man, paid for by Warner Brothers,
Who drives me to work.
See that?! I didn't want to say it . . .
I HAVE A DRIVER.
And yes, it's as strange as it sounds.
He comes around to open my door.

At first, I objected,
But now I see it as it is:
I want to be my best at my work
And he at his.
We play our roles.

In his car, I used to
Force a conversation
To disguise us as
Just two guys carpooling.

Now we mostly sit in silence
Unless we *have* to talk.
Like last night,
When he said, "I wouldn't want that job,"
As we passed a prostitute
In stilettos and fishnets
Shivering on the sidewalk in the snow.

MARDER

I'm quarantined in Chicago
In a freezing February Airbnb
Feeling sorry for me as I
Recover from left hip surgery.

I got an email from an old college friend.
"I know you knew Andreas from basketball," he wrote.
"His wife wanted me to let people know
He passed away this week. Still only in his forties."

Earlier this morning, I read a Mary Oliver poem
About her friend Tom, who died.
He had decades kept her warm, she wrote,
A "friendship always as beautiful as a flame."

You, Dar, and all our growing up together came to mind,
And the icy tears years from now,
When you or I will die before the other.
The bone-chilling cold
Of being in this world without you.

MEN IN WOODS

My new friend proposed
A day and night of camping—
"Sleeping under the stars," he called it.
And I wondered, maybe worried just a bit:
Would he try to kiss me again?
Did he want to hike with me because he liked me?
Or was it that he *liked* me?

How triumphant I felt on our twelve-mile
Walk along the ridges, when we talked about
How we hoped to start a band,
And when I laughed and called him a "whiner"
For his complaints about his knee
(And the altitude and the heat).

We both wore old sneakers and slipped on the trail.
And when we skinny-dipped in a shallow stream,
We noticed, each in the other's body,
That our grown-man bellies didn't match our
Boyish downhill jogs.

In the car, when I asked who the music was,
He turned it up, showing off
The speakers in his new car.
We listened, wind-chapped, to the CD.
He's going to burn me a copy.

The parents

HOUSEKEEPING

For the first time in three years,
I've come, from California to the New England hills,
To see my mother
For just two days.
She lives alone, and the wood floors in her house
Have swollen and buckled
From the summer's endless humidity.
She called me to her room tonight:
"Come look. Come see."
I stopped in the doorway,
Watched her toss treats to her dog,
So proud when he would catch and chew.
Her room strewn with clothes,
The blond dog misses:
"What's the matter, Buttercup?
You're so tired."
And she kneels down
On the stained blue carpet,
Already forgetting I am there.

OLD BONES

This morning,
The smell of bacon
Brought me downstairs,
But before I reached
The open kitchen door,
A voice stopped me.

My mother telling
Her old, arthritic dog,
"I know sweetness,
You've been carrying those bones
For a long time."

I leaned unseen
On the mildewed windowsill,
Watching her
Sip coffee,
Fry bacon,

Her old dog
Pressing at her knee.

THE FLY

My mother, sixty-three, has lost weight
And looks happy when I see her.

Yesterday, for her birthday surprise, we took her sailing.
She sailed with her father in the '50s,
Won a regatta with him when she was seventeen.

Our aging captain has earrings and a nose ring
And hops boyishly on board.
He's so happy that we came
And tells us which is the jib and which the mainsail.

When he bends to take a line
His unzipped fly folds open,
And I see his penis swing out.
I say nothing
Because he's tucked his shirt in today
And worn nice shoes
And wants us to notice
How well-kept his boat is.

Since I was four,
I've been parent to my little world,
Taking care of mom and brother,
Taking pains not to
Rub anyone the wrong way
Or make them feel bad,
No matter how bad I feel.

Now I'm in my forties
And I can't even say,
"Hey man, your fly's undone."

TAXI

There's this long cab ride
After she's stayed with me
Four days for her birthday.
She's sixty-two.
She inhales to gather courage in the cab
To broach the big stuff
Before she flies away.

All weekend, she's been telling big stories
Full of hyperbole, maybe hoping,
If she opens her eyes wide
And gestures wildly enough,
That that parade of it all might ignite me.

I read it takes an atomic bomb
To trigger a hydrogen bomb.
This visit, she's been Nagasaki
While I've been a cool four-day drizzle.
When I hear myself speak,
I don't recognize the boy;
I'm somewhere else,
A bored tour guide,
Waiting for the weekend's end.

In the cab,
She's just finished telling me
She hopes I still have children someday.

I tap the vinyl of the seat next to me,
And, mistaking it for a reach,
She takes my hand.

I freeze, then squeeze back
And whisper, "I love you."

TOWN CAR

When I was a kid, my mother collected food stamps.
Now I complain that she brags about me too much.
There's a photo on her mantle of the president and me.
She tells everyone who visits that I've been on TV
And published poems. It nettles at me.

Last night, I made dinner on my new, high-end barbecue grill
For my mother and her two friends.
I lit candles, but when she started to say,
In a stagelike whisper,
That I built this fine home, with its high skylights,
I halted her with a singsong teenage "Mom!"

This morning, we both had flights, so in a fancy gesture
I took her to the airport in a tinted town car
With a pinstriped driver who held her cane.
Sitting next to me,
She told me she wished we had a
Better connection
And that she no longer thought my wife wasn't
Good enough
But still hoped she would make me a father someday.

And I thought:
Maybe she isn't so impressed by the car
And by the driver
And the legroom and the leather.
All wasted.
And now I'm hours early for my flight.

THE DRIVER

Crossing Maine in his minivan in the dark
To a town called Bath,
We never knew what to say to one another.
We pass lighted lobster shacks and outlet malls,
The sound of wet tires on highway
Fills in for the unspoken words.

He munches steadily through a
Big bag of Doritos.
He's always had something
Crunchy at the ready on the road.

He's always had a van too.
I remember, at three or four, staring up at his
Fingers wrapped around the wheel,
His face weighted with loneliness,
Just before my mom
Moved us away from him.
Peanuts rattling
In the console on the dash.

Now, sitting here full grown,
I'm staring still at his big hands.
Knowing that they'll keep me safe.

The kids

BABY PANTS*

I drive across town for a friend
To Justin's house on a Saturday at 9 A.M.
His wife, belt unbuckled, yells for him from under wet hair.
He's down in the office,
And I collapse on the new couch,
Custom made, brown and squarer than a couch should be.

Justin's baby produces baby pants for my inspection.
I'm impressed that he can find his own pants now.
Can't put them on but knows they go
On his baby legs.

And there I am with my friend's family
On another weekend morning.
The mother holds an envelope in her teeth,
Hoists and struggles to pant her boy.

I'm slouching hot in my vest,
My blue down vest,
Thinking today was colder than it is.
Forgetting that fall in California
Is like summer back home.

Plastic diapers pack the thighs of tiny corduroys.
The smell of Cheerios bloated and floating in milk.
What have I missed?

*This is the first poem I ever wrote.

THE VISIT

My godson's dad
Lives in Michigan,
Doesn't answer the phone.

Little Joey came to
Visit me at work yesterday.
We ate pork tacos;
He desserted on Yoplait.

On the drive home,
He told his mom
It was the best day of his life.

So I am a six-year-old's man:
Two little eyes watching me
To see how he should be.

JUNK MAIL

The tenants at my old house
Saved my mail in a box—
Returned Christmas cards,
Expired Home Depot coupons,
And a copy of *Pearl*,
A poetry journal, with
A thing about flowering trees
Written by me.
I reread it in the kitchen
Over the open box of bulk mail.
It says that my wife
Has been waiting for the trees to flower
Or maybe for something else,
And now twenty years after we first kissed
We have a baby on the way.
Maybe this
Is what we've been waiting on
All these years?

THE SEAL

We're calling it "The Seal"
Because last week
The sonogram
Had a fishlike look
When we saw the pixelated
Heartbeat on the screen.

A new doctor has squeezed us in
On short notice because of the bleeding.
Standing with forceps in her scrubs,
She does not trade in comfort.
She talks of biopsies, irregularities, and worst cases.

I squeeze your hand and wipe the hair
That has sweated to your face.
You look to me, cheeks swollen with fear;
I try to soothe with a flat joke,
"Quite a party, huh?"
I steady the spinning room
By pressing the table with my knee.

THE NEST

One clung sleeping to your chest,
Another climbed from the empty hamper,
Hair blue and wet, declaring, "Upside Up!"

Tonight, our minds race
Side by side,
The broken day of the broken dishwasher,
And I have to fly back to Canada tomorrow.

When will sleep ever meet us?
Can we find, on our 22nd Valentine's,
Twenty conjugal minutes?
Or will we lie
In this heap of little bodies,
Worrying the dark away?

PRESENT. TENSE.

Their mother is two days away for the first time,
And we are midway through our first afternoon.
I'm standing impatient on the grass near other new parents
As my five-year-old, West, dangles his weight
From a toy steering wheel bolted to the slide.
"Chase me, Dad!"
But I'm seeing what important things
Have happened on my iPhone.

I remember when I was small,
Taking my father's big fingers,
Gripping them in my little fist,
And feeling invincible.

Maison, my toddler, is yawning in the wood chips,
So I give the "five-minute warning"
Because I've read that small children have
Hard times with transitions.
Their days, of course, are packed with transitions,
So their life is filled with anxious warnings
From adults who always want them to be
Somewhere other than where they are.

I'm ready for the next thing, ready to be done with slides.
And besides, their five minutes are up, so
I tug them by the hands to our minivan in the parking lot,
And as I'm buckling Maison in her car seat,
She sees a flower on the curb that's gone to seed.

"Dad, I want the dandelion,"
In her three-year-old dialect.
Sighing, I stoop and pick one for each of us
And one for the absent mother.
And congratulate myself on my patience.

I ask my son to make a wish for his mom.
I say, "Maybe a long, happy life."
He blows dandelion for his mother into the car.
I think of the mess, of how the little seeds will stick to the seats.
Then he blows his own wish:
"I wish for a baby leopard."

Walking around the car, I make my own wish
That I won't wake up someday and wonder where my life went,
That I will somehow find my way to happiness.

And now it's Maison's turn.
She starts pulling the white fluff off with her fingers.
I say, "No, no, sweetie," and West explains:
"You have to puff it and make a wish."
Then she smilingly blows the wisps from off the stem,
And as they float toward me, she says,
"I wish for this."

THE LAST POEM

My seven-year-old still crawls out of his bed and into ours
Every night between eleven and three.
The relocation wakes his little sister, and she comes too,
 Crying, still half-dreaming, down the unlit hall.
"Mama, Dadda, where are you?!"
"Right here, little one. In bed. In our bed.
 Where we always are."

Four rib-jabbing, perpendicular little legs.
Coughs and whimpers in the dark.
My daughter soothes herself terribly
By fingernail-pinching my nipples.

After an hour or two of fitful wrestling in our nest,
Warmth and wetness wake me.
I get one of our thick, gray towels, spread it
Across the pee-damped portion of the sheets,
And try angrily to find a way to get back to my sleep.

But this morning, far from home,
I wake alone in my own rented bed, revived by rest.
This, I think, *is what it feels like to have slept.*
And I decide that upon return I will announce:
"The children are old enough—past due
 To sleep in their own beds.
 We can't live as ghosts like this!"

Lying there in the quiet and the still
For longer than I have in years
In this empty room with
One little window,
I drift to those half-naked, warm little ones
Nuzzling under my grown-man arms,
Making pillows of my shoulders,
Recounting the sounds of their sleep,
Sniffle-snoring through those tiny, runny little noses.

And I wonder:
What have I missed?
One night soon they will sigh their last
Sleeping breath of childhood,
And when they do,
I want to be pressed close and alert
To breathe it in and hold it
In my body forever.

INDEX

ACKNOWLEDGMENTS

This is the near-end page where I list the people who helped me write this book. First, I want to thank the people I love who are mentioned in these poems as well as the handful of people who read my manuscript and gave me notes (there is overlap between the two groups). I also want to note that there are people I love—my sisters, Danielle and Liz, my Sasha, Philip, Susan, and my grandmother, to name a few—who deserve whole chapters in the book of my life, but whom I did not substantially write about in these pages.

Many of my poems are about my wife—the most important grown-up in my life. After thirty years together, we have separated, but she will always be woven into the fabric of me, and I am forever grateful for her. I cried many times rereading the pages about her. My love for her will always remain.

Thank you to Matt Thomas, my dear college friend and an incredible author, who encouraged me and patiently worked through early drafts line by line, comma by comma.

Thank you to Karina White, my longtime creative collaborator for her cover design and photo of the LA skyline and for her friendship and devotion to font perfection.

Thank you to my agents, Byrd Leavell and Meredith Miller, who worked hard to find this book the best publishing team even though books of poems have made no agent any dollars, ever. Thank you to Patty Rice, my editor, whom it feels like

I've known my whole life after just three months, and thank you to everyone at Andrews McMeel Publishing.

I also want to thank my mother and father. The poems in this book don't highlight the virtues of my childhood, but when I was small, my parents tricked me into believing that I could do whatever I wanted with my life and that I deserved to be listened to. Thank you for that subterfuge.

And finally, thank you, West and Maison. Some days I feel that my whole purpose in being was to share this life with you. Watching you grow is my greatest happiness.

Andrews McMeel Publishing
a division of Andrews McMeel Universal
1130 Walnut Street, Kansas City, Missouri 64106

www.andrewsmcmeel.com

21 22 23 24 25 VEP 10 9 8 7 6 5 4 3 2

ISBN: 978-1-5248-7054-6

Library of Congress Control Number: 2021940504

Editor: Patty Rice
Art Director: Spencer Williams
Production Editor: Elizabeth A. Garcia
Production Manager: Cliff Koehler

Cover photo and design by Karina White
Author photo by Monica D. Photography

"Baby Pants" and "Old Bones" appeared in *Columbia Poetry Review,*
no. 21, Spring 2008.

"Black Cat" and "Suddenly" appeared in *Columbia Poetry Review,*
no. 32, Spring 2019.

"June Second" appeared in *Pearl,* Issue 41, 2009.

"Reread" appeared in *California Quarterly,* Volume 34, no. 1.

ATTENTION: SCHOOLS AND BUSINESSES
Andrews McMeel books are available at quantity discounts with bulk
purchase for educational, business, or sales promotional use. For information,
please e-mail the Andrews McMeel Publishing Special Sales Department:
specialsales@amuniversal.com.